Challenge

Englisch für Berufliche Gymnasien Klasse 11

Workbook

von
Andrea Eder-Panev
Anne Herlyn
Annely Humphreys
Jason Humphreys
Ephrem Wellenbrock (Hrsg.)

Ernst Klett Verlag
Stuttgart • Leipzig

Bundesausgabe

1. Auflage 1 5 4 3 2 1 | 24 23 22 21 20

Alle Drucke dieser Auflage sind unverändert und können im Unterricht nebeneinander verwendet werden.
Die letzte Zahl bezeichnet das Jahr des Druckes.

Herausgeber: Ephrem Wellenbrock, Dorsten
Autorinnen und Autoren: Andrea Eder-Panev, Leipzig; Anne Herlyn, Waldkirch; Annely und Jason Humphreys, Frickenhofen; Ephrem Wellenbrock, Dorsten

Entstanden in Zusammenarbeit mit dem Projektteam des Verlages

Umschlaggestaltung: Gourdin & Müller GbR, Leipzig
Gestaltungskonzept: Gourdin & Müller GbR, Leipzig
Umschlagfoto: Adobe Stock (FS-Stock), Dublin
Illustrationen: Koma Amok, Stuttgart; Matthias Pflügner, Berlin
Satz: Druckmedienzentrum Gotha GmbH, Gotha
Reproduktion: Schwabenrepro GmbH, Stuttgart
Druck: Gebr. Geiselberger GmbH, Altötting

Printed in Germany
ISBN 978-3-12-809282-9

9 783128 092829

Symbole

A1 Audioverweis

→ SB p. 1 Verweise auf das Schülerbuch Challenge, Klasse 11

→ S 10.1 Verweis auf die *Skills files* im Schülerbuch

→ Talking about . . . Verweis auf Online-Grammatik mit Erklärfilmen und Übungen

Für die Grammatik-Erklärfilme sowie die Übungen dazu, geben Sie den Code **2iq4e4** unter www.klett.de ein.

Die Audio-Dateien, Audioskripte und die Lösungen finden Sie auch online.
Geben Sie einfach den Challenge-Code **3rq4bb** unter www.klett.de ein.

Being young

1 Thinking about the future → SB, pp. 18–19

a Match the terms below to the headings (1.–6.). Then add two of your own ideas to each heading.

having a secure job | having close friends | being politically active | having children | keeping fit | being in a long-term relationship | living in a safe area | protecting the environment | progressing in one's career | enjoying one's job | fearing unemployment | finding affordable housing | eating healthily | fearing terror attacks | doing voluntary work | having interesting hobbies

1. Personal relationships

   having close friends ____________________

   ____

   ____

   ____

2. Safety and stability

   ____

   ____

   ____

   ____

3. Social engagement

   ____

   ____

   ____

   ____

4. Work and career

   ____

   ____

   ____

   ____

5. Health and life style

   ____

   ____

   ____

   ____

6. Fears and worries

   ____

   ____

   ____

   ____

b Using the ideas from a, write 3 – 4 sentences about what will be important to you in the future.

____
____
____
____
____
____
____
____

2 Focus on grammar → SB, p.19 → Talking about the future

Complete the sentences using the correct form of the future. Give the reason for the form you have chosen.

1. Perhaps in the future, finding affordable housing *will be difficult* (to be difficult).
   Reason: *prediction/assumption = will-future*
2. I ______________________ (to play football) tomorrow at 7 a.m.
   Reason: ______________________
3. We ______________________ (to have children) when we are married.
   Reason: ______________________
4. Maybe she ______________________ (to study) economics at university.
   Reason: ______________________
5. He's very smart and his boss likes him. He's definitely ______________________ (to progress in one's career).
   Reason: ______________________
6. We ____________ (to need to) tighten security measures during the tournament next week to reduce the risk of terror attacks.
   Reason: ______________________
7. I hope I ______________________ (to still have) lots of close friends after I have left university.
   Reason: ______________________
8. We ____________ (to build) a big house in the countryside. We've already bought the land.
   Reason: ______________________
9. If it rains, maybe they ______________________ (to go to the cinema) instead.
   Reason: ______________________
10. What ____________ you ______________________ (to do) during the summer holidays?
    Reason: ______________________

1 Working with a cartoon → SB, p. 21 → S 10.3

a Describe the cartoon.

b What message does the cartoon want to convey?

c What is your opinion on the topic of the cartoon?

2 Listening: Students' online habits → SB, p. 22

A1

a Listen to the radio programme and answer the following questions.

1. How many students took part in the survey? ______
2. How was participation encouraged? ______

b Listen again and fill in the table with information from the radio programme.

What positive aspects does the internet offer to students?	*– research and learning*
What negative aspects does the internet present?	
What possible strategies are there to reduce time on social media?	
What are the arguments against these strategies?	

A Style and life style

1 Crossword puzzle → SB, pp. 23 – 24

Across (→)
3. large group of people
4. truthful
5. unique
6. strong belief
9. supportive
10. to win

Down (↓)
1. really
2. considered as normal
7. label
8. idea

2 Focus on grammar: Asking questions → SB, pp. 23 – 24 → Talking about the present

The text about Reese Blutstein is the result of an interview.
Which questions did the interviewer ask her to get the following information?

1. began her social media account at 18
____
____

2. born in 1997
____

3. Atlanta-based
____

4. shares her outfits on her blog
____

5. has fans around the world
____

6. receives regular collaboration offers from different brands
____

7. looks at online platforms for inspiration
____

8. has 200,00 followers
____

3 Word webs → SB, pp. 23–24

Complete the following word webs with related words from the text about Reese Blutstein.

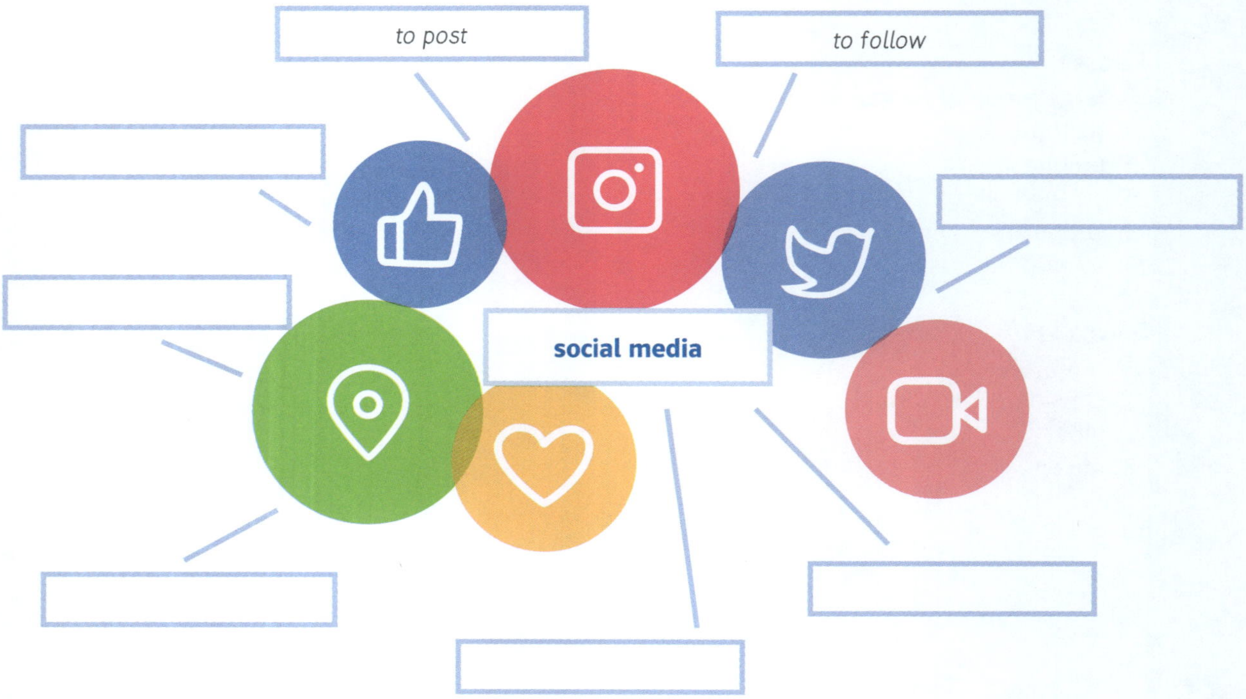

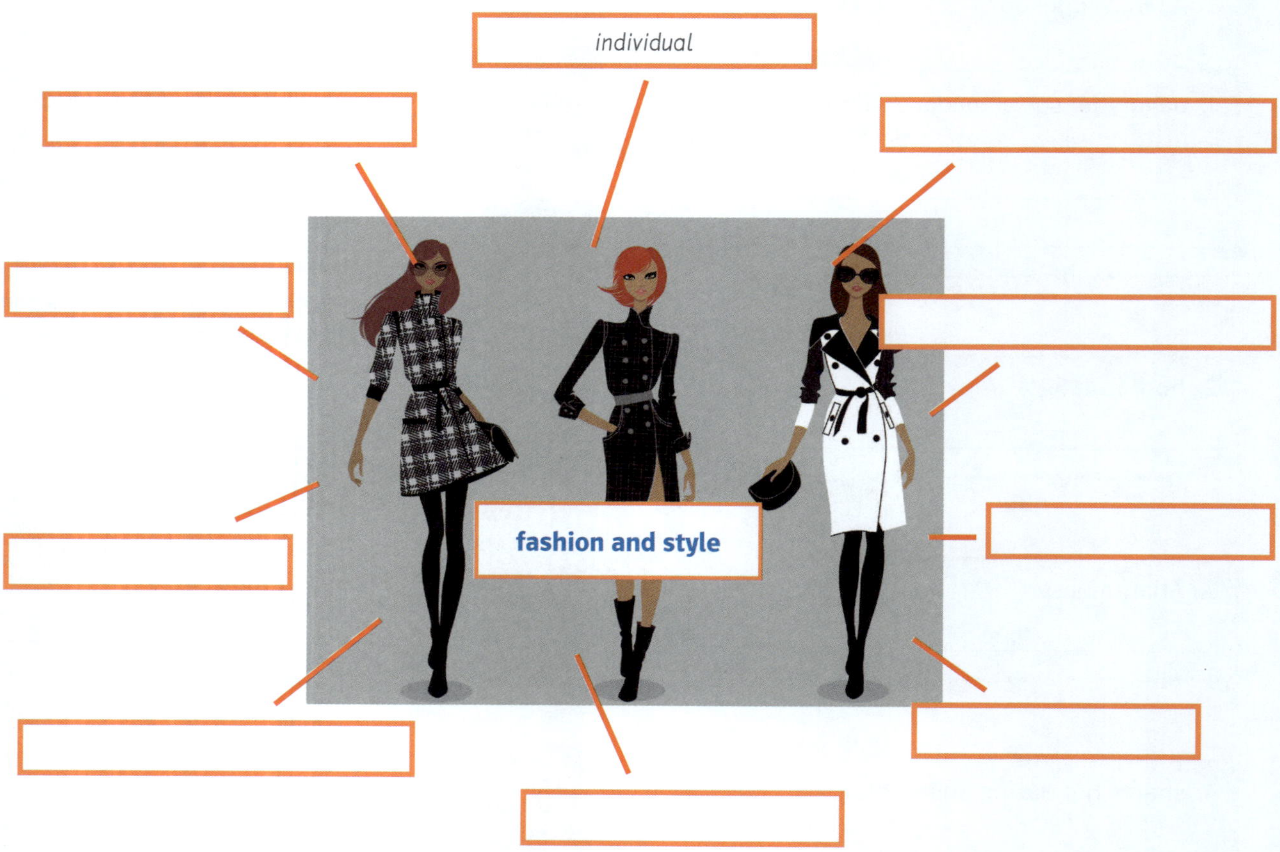

4 Style adjectives → SB, pp. 23 – 26

Match the adjectives in the table to the descriptions below and think of an example for which occasion you might wear each style.

arty, wild patterns and textures | comfortable, informal | simple, athletic clothes such as sweatpants, t-shirts and trainers | tailored items, suits | clothes typical of a certain country or culture | elegant, high quality

Style	Description	Example occasion
sporty		
classic		
traditional		
casual		
formal		
hippy		

5 Writing a short text: My style → SB, pp. 23 – 26

Now use the words from exercises 3 and 4 to describe your own style. Does social media influence what you wear?

B A different kind of reality

1 Listening: The British accent → SB, pp. 27–30 → S 2

A2

a Before you listen, explain what is meant by the phrase: "Whereas a British accent used to be the hallmark of a movie villain, these days it is seen as more redolent of class and wit." (ll. 84–86)

____

____

____

b Listen to the conversation with a specalist on British accents and answer the following questions.

1. In which kinds of films do actors often use the British accent and what is it often associated with?

____

____

2. Which accents were considered attractive? Note them down in the order of their attractiveness.

I. ______________ III. ______________

II. ______________ IV. ______________

3. What qualities does the British accent convey in everyday life? (3 words)

____

4. Name the two situations mentioned where the British accent achieves better results.

____

____

5. Who speaks the Queen's English?

____

6. What can you say about the number of dialects on the British Isles and in North America?

____

2 Explain the following phrases. → SB, p. 28

four-legged variety (ll. 11–12) ______________________________

____

survival-type shows (ll. 35–36) ______________________________

____

on-screen personality (ll. 47–48) ______________________________

____

self-rescue skills (l. 64) ______________________________

____

ever-present nostalgia (l. 73) ______________________________

____

3 **Find headlines for the following paragraphs.** → SB, p. 28

5–21: ______________________

22–45: ______________________

46–58: ______________________

59–82: ______________________

59–66: ______________________

67–82: ______________________

83–89: ______________________

4 **Write a summary with the help of your headlines from ex. 3.** → SB, p. 28

____

____

____

____

____

5 **Focus on grammar: The passive** → SB, p. 30 → Talking about processes

Use the correct form of the passive.

Bear Grylls show ____________ 1 (criticize) for misleading scenes which were deliberately dramatized or even fake. In an episode of his show in 2017, Bear Grylls and US dance star Derek Hough ____________ 2 (show) killing and boiling a frog before swimming across a lake in the Bulgarian Rila mountains, which ____________ 3 (forbid). The Rila National Park in southwestern Bulgaria is the country's largest. It ____________ 4 (protect) and the Bulgarian ministry said the crew ____________ 5 (inform) on what they could not do during the filming. It is still unclear if Bear Grylls ____________ 6 (punish) for his actions during the filming.

6 **Focus on grammar: The personal passive** → SB, p. 30 → Talking about processes

Change the following sentences into personal passive using the words in brackets.

1. Many people believe that Bear Grylls has a net worth of around £6 million. (believe)

   ____

2. Many people think that Grylls is one of the youngest men to climb Mount Everest. (think)

   ____

3. More celebrities will probably take part in this exciting TV show. (assume)

   ____

4. Grylls might start the new season of "Running Wild with Bear Grylls" next summer. (suppose)

   ____

5. With this show Grylls might collect a lot of money for children's charities. (expect)

   ____

C Family

1 Reading for detail
→ SB, pp. 31 – 32

Think of a heading for each of the following 7 sections from the extract from David Nicholls' *Us*.

	Section	Heading
1.	ll. 3 – 6	*First encounter in the breakfast room*
2.	ll. 7 – 10	
3.	ll. 12 – 20	
4.	ll. 25 – 29	
5.	ll. 30 – 34	
6.	ll. 41 – 43	
7.	ll. 44 – 45	

2 Reading for detail: Cause and effect
→ SB, pp. 31 – 32

In the scene in the breakfast room, the characters often react to something another person said or did. Find these examples and fill in the cause or effect.

Cause	→ Effect
Albie and Cat are kissing when his parents first arrive	→ Douglas has a bad first impression of Cat
	→ Albie is uncomfortable and embarrassed
Cat takes more from the breakfast buffet than is acceptable	→
Douglas openly criticises Cat	→
	→ Albie's mother speaks to him sternly

3 Describing pictures
→ S 10.1

Write a description of the picture. What sort of atmosphere does it show?

D Living abroad

1 True or false? →SB, p. 36

Read the following statements and say if they are true or false. Correct the false statements.

	True	False
1. Kate French did not want to find a long-term job in London.		
2. Many of her friends had taken gap years to work abroad.		
3. Kate had relatives with whom she could stay in Australia.		
4. She first started working in an area where there were many holidaymakers.		
5. Eventually she got her first job in Australia at a bank.		
6. She asked her manager to help her with her job application documents.		
7. Kate was much more positive after her experiences working in Australia.		

2 Words matter → SB, p. 36

Explain the following terms from the text in your own words.

1. to commit to something (l. 4): ______
2. to go for it (l. 7): ______
3. to get disheartened (l. 12): ______
4. to walk into something (l. 14): ______
5. to hit the ground running (ll. 27–28): ______
6. to be put forward for something (l. 40): ______

3 Mediation → SB, p. 37

Match the German terms from the text to the English equivalent.

1. sich um etwas handeln
2. in der Regel
3. Erfahrungen sammeln
4. Vorurteil
5. ein Gespür für etwas bekommen
6. etwas über Bord werfen
7. reichen
8. anders herum

A to gain experience
B to get a feel for something
C to concern something
D prejudice
E the other way around
F to abandon something
G generally
H to be enough

Teens and screens → SB, pp. 40 – 41

1 Read the text and say if the following statements are true or false. Correct the false statements.

Statement	True	False
1. Young people should not spend more than four hours a day in front of a small screen.		
2. One effect of too much screen time can be social isolation.		
3. A possible physical effect of too much screen time can be weight loss.		
4. Teens should be physically active for at least 30 – 60 minutes a day.		
5. Too much screen time can have both physical and mental effects.		

2 To prepare assignment 1 in your student book, collect the physical and mental effects of too much screen time that are mentioned in the text.

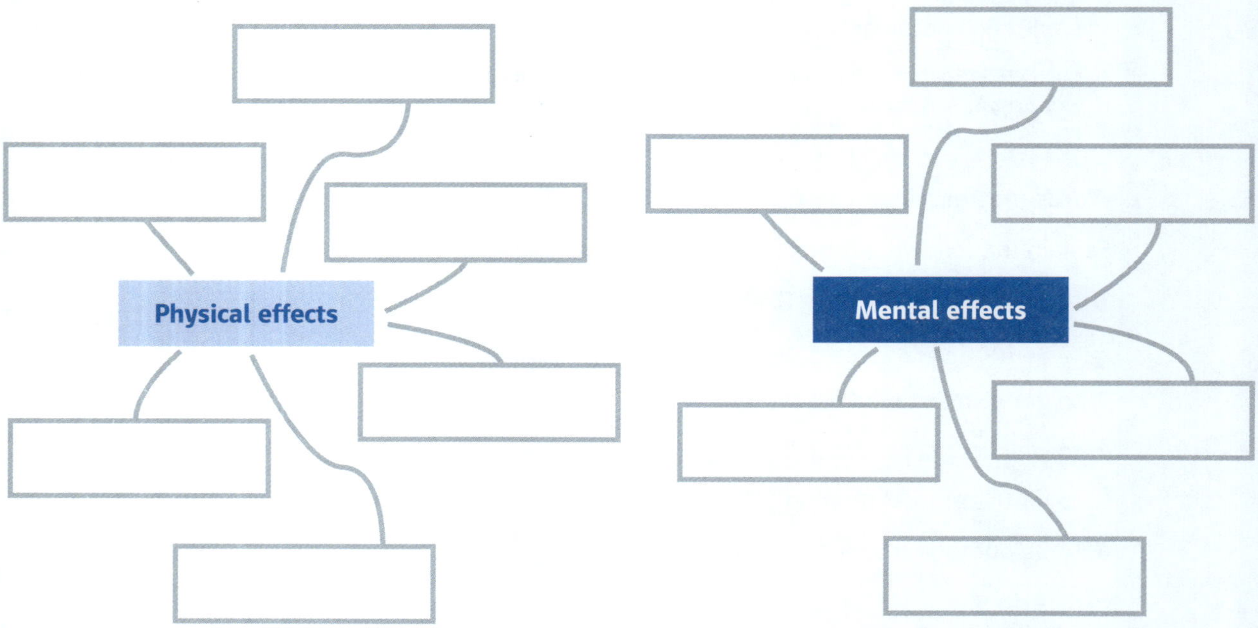

3 Complete the sentences about the tips for limiting screen time using the connectives below.

in addition | finally | moreover | furthermore | then | first of all | for example

1. ______________________, physical activity is very important.
2. ______________________, parents should talk to their children and teach them about the consequences of too much screen time.
3. ______________________, they should make screen time a reward!
4. ______________________, parents can ask their children to concentrate on one thing and not practice multi-tasking.
5. ________________, there are more tips, ____________________ days without screen time, no screens during meals, and just a little screen time in the bedroom.
6. ______________________, it is important for parents to be convincing role models!

4 Find suitable phrases in lines 1–31 for the following definitions.

1. keep the same level ______
2. rise significantly ______
3. the position when you stand, sit … ______
4. something is getting worse ______
5. the changes how somebody feels ______
6. being absent from school without excuse ______

5 The text gives different suggestions how to use digital media sensibly (ll. 36–91). Analyse critically how you should change your behaviour and write down what measures you personally will/should take.

1. ______
2. ______
3. ______
4. ______
5. ______

6 Describing and analysing a cartoon. → S 10.3

Describe and analyse the cartoon. Comment on the difference between communication styles of the older and younger generations. → S 10.3

The experience of work

1 Talking about your job → SB, p. 42

a An online career blog is collecting personal accounts of people's jobs. Read Pascal's text and fill in the missing words.

Pascal, 28, industrial engineer

clients | variety | working language | got used to it | efficient | manufacturing | hands-on | software | main tasks | improve | math | reduce

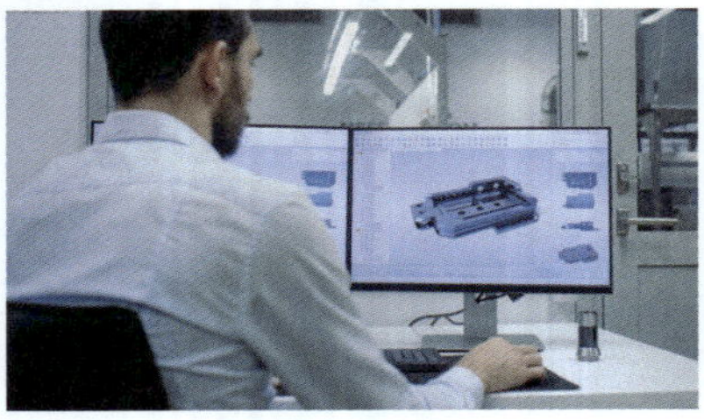

I work for a large ________________ 1 company in Hamburg but I travel a lot, particularly to the USA and China, where we have important __________ 2. One of my __________________ 3 is looking at ways to ___________ 4 the production process and how to minimise waste and make things more _____________ 5. I work with some very advanced computer _______________ 6, which is great for me as I'm a bit of a computer geek. There is also quite a bit of __________ 7 involved as I have to deal with a lot of data and financial issues, in particular how to ____________ 8 costs. My job is also very _____________ 9, so I need to be fit. Even though I work for a German company, our _____________________ 10 is English. That was a little strange at the beginning, but I __________________ 11 very quickly. The best thing about my job is the ____________ 12. Every day there is another problem to solve!

b Use the key words to write a text about Freya's work.

Freya, 29, self-employed art therapist

social skills | creativity | patience | self-expression | rewarding | working with people | passion for art | administrative tasks | writing reports | financial planning

Hi, I'm Freya. ______________________________________

____

____

____

____

____

____

____

____

1 Letter of application and CV → SB, p. 44 → S 12.2, 12.3, 12.4

In order to improve your English skills, you are looking for an internship at a British company for the summer holidays. You have found the following job advertisement online and decide to apply for one of the positions advertised.

Swift Sports

We are a leading British sports equipment manufacturer and are looking for young reliable students from Europe to do work placements (4–6 weeks) in our offices and production plants in London, Birmingham and Manchester. We offer positions in the following areas of work:

- Manufacturing Department
- Sales Department
- Nursery school for our employees' children

If you are interested in one of these areas and you are aged 16–24, then send your application and a full CV to our personnel manager, Ms Claudia Ainsworth at

c.ainsworth@swiftsports.ldn

a Read the job advertisement and fill in the email below with your own ideas. Use the letter of application in your student book (p. 44) to help you.

From:	...
To:	c.ainsworth@swiftsports.ldn
Subject:	Work Placement Application
Attachments:	CV.pdf

Dear Ms Ainsworth
With reference to the work placement advert on your website, I would like to apply for a position in ...

b Now complete this CV with information about yourself.

Curriculum Vitae

Name ______________________________

Address ______________________________

____

____

Phone ______________________________

Email ______________________________

Date of birth ______________________________

Nationality ______________________________

Personal statement ______________________________

____

____

____

____

Education ______________________________

____

____

____

____

Work experience ______________________________

____

____

____

Skills ______________________________

____

____

____

____

____

A Choosing a career

1 Focus on sentences → SB, pp. 47 – 48

Scan the text and find out what the following numbers refer to.
Write whole sentences and try to use your own words as much as possible.

13 – 17 *Ernst & Young and Junior Achievement researched the career choices of 13- to 17-year-olds.*

91 ____________________

36 ____________________

11 ____________________

28 ____________________

25 ____________________

85 ____________________

73 ____________________

54 ____________________

50 ____________________

B Applying for a job

1 Focus on grammar: If-clauses

→ SB, pp. 50–52 → Talking about conditions

a Use the words to make sentences with if-clauses, type 1. Pay attention to whether they are positive, negative, or a question.

1. you / prepare for the interview / it / go well

   If you prepare ... ______

2. you / be unprepared / the interviewers / notice

   ______

3. you / arrive late / you / not make a good first impression

   ______

4. they / want to know your weaknesses / they / ask

   ______

5. you / not ask any questions / you / look uninterested in the position

   ______

6. what / you say / they ask about / your weaknesses

   ______

b Two students are talking about career choices.
Complete their conversation by including the correct if-clause, types 1 or 2.

Student 1: I think I'd like to start my own business one day.

Student 2: Really! Why?

Student 1: Well, if I start my own business, I ______ 1 (to be) my own boss. And if I ______ 2 (to be) my own boss, I could do what I wanted.

Student 2: That's true, but if you ______ 3 (to not have) a good idea, your company won't be successful.

Student 1: Sure, but I do have a few ideas. And if just one of them worked out, I ______ 4 (to have) a good chance of being successful.

Student 2: I suppose if your company ______ 5 (to be successful), you'll make a lot of money, but I don't think I want to be an entrepreneur.

Student 1: Why not?

Student 2: I just think that if you ______ 6 (to work) for a large company, you will have more job security.

Student 1: That could be true, but I think if I ______ 7 (to work) for a big company, I would get bored quickly. On the other hand, If I had my own start-up, I ______ 8 (to enjoy) going to work every morning.

c Rewrite the sentences to form negative statements.

1. Theresa has a lot of job interview experience. She feels relaxed.

   If Theresa didn't have a lot of job experience, she wouldn't ...

2. I am well prepared for the interview. I am very confident.

3. The company is growing fast. There are good opportunities for me.

4. My CV looks good. I will send it off to the company.

d Two friends are chatting about jobs and careers. Use their answers to write the questions using if-clauses, type 2.

1.

   Oh, good question. If I could work anywhere, I would work in Australia, I think.

2.

   Hmmm, I think if money wasn't important, I would work in a kangaroo sanctuary, or something like that.

3.

   That's easy. If I could choose a company car, I would choose an electric car.

e Use if-clauses type 3 to make positive statements from the negative statements below.

1. The interview didn't go well. I didn't get the job.

   If the interview had gone well, ...

2. I missed my bus. I didn't make it to the interview on time.

3. I didn't want to work for a large company. I turned down the job offer.

4. I didn't have the right skills. I was not suitable for the job.

C Dealing with customers

A3

1 Listening: Taking a message

Listen to the conversation between Sabine and a customer who wishes to talk to her boss, Mr Brown.

a What is Mr Canfield's problem?

____

____

b How does Sabine offer to help?

____

____

2 Words matter

There are many different ways to describe and give additional information on how something is said. Match the words to the correct definition in the table below.

acknowledge | admit | claim | deny | enquire (about something) | express | state | stress | promise | offer

Verb	Definition
	to say that you are willing to do something
	to say, possibly against your will, that you have done something, or that something is true
	to say that you think something is not true
	to say that something is true, although there is no proof of it
	to agree that something exists or is true
	to emphasise something and show that it is important
	to say that you are definitely going to do something
	to say your opinion formally
	to show what you are thinking (using words, looks or actions)
	to ask (about something)

3 Focus on sentences

Later, Sabine wants to tell Mr Brown about the phone call. Use words from the exercise above to complete the dialogue.

Sabine: Good afternoon, Mr Brown. I wanted to let you know that while you were away, a customer from Office & School called and ______________ 1 about the status of his order.

Mr Brown: Oh, hi Sabine. Thanks for taking the message. Which customer was it?

Sabine: Mr Canfield. I asked for his customer ID, but he ______________ 2 that he didn't have it on him. He ______________ 3 that you would know where to place him if I told you his name.

Mr Brown: Ah yes, now I remember. And what is the problem, exactly?

Sabine: Well, he ______________ 4 that he made an offer for a shipment of folders three weeks ago, but hasn't received it or heard anything since.

Mr Brown: Hmm, that is strange. I will have to look into that.

Sabine: He ______________ 5 his concern about the matter and ______________ 6 that it was really important for him to get the folders soon.

Mr Brown: All right. What did you tell him?

Sabine: I ______________ 7 that I would let you know about it as soon as you got in. I ______________ 8 to try and reach you on your mobile phone, but he didn't think that that was necessary.

Mr Brown: OK. I'll check the status right away and give him a call. Thanks, Sabine.

4 Focus on Grammar → SB, p. 56 → Talking about passing on information

Watch the video "Ordering goods" again. After the telephone conversation, Jennifer Davis tells her boss, Ms Thompson, what Mr Cooper said about the following topics. Construct sentences using indirect speech.

1. the colour "bored banana"

   He said that it was a good choice and ______________________________

   ____

2. a discount

   ____

3. the total price of the order after the discount

   ____

4. the payment date

   ____

5. the time of delivery

   ____

6. greetings to Ms Thompson

   ____

D Going your own way

1 Listening: The gig economy → SB, pp. 58–60 → S 2

A4

a Before you listen: What do you think the gig economy is? Choose the right option.

The gig economy is …

A ☐ an economy in which independent workers are offered temporary or short-term employment.

B ☐ an economy with an usually high level of unemployment.

C ☐ another name for Industry 4.0.

b Listen to the conversation for the first time and answer the following questions.

1. What is the gig economy?

____

____

2. What does Helen say about the kind of jobs in the gig economy?

____

____

____

____

3. Why did Jack start his blog?

____

____

____

____

4. Why did Jack go to university?

____

____

____

5. What are the advantages of the gig economy for workers? Name three things.

____

____

____

____

6. How do companies find freelancers?

____

____

7. Why does Helen call people in the gig economy "disposable workers"?

8. How does the gig economy support entrepreneurship? Name two things.

c Now listen again and fill in the details about the different gig economy workers you hear from.

Name	Job(s)	Reason(s) for working in the gig economy	Likes/dislikes the gig economy because …
Jack			
Jenny			
Julian			

d What about you? Could you work in the gig economy? If so, what kind of work would you do and why? And if not, why not?

A Harvest of Thorns → SB, p.63

1 Reading for detail

1. Name the fields of work in which immigrants from Bangladesh could work in (in a country such as Malaysia).

   ____

2. Explain what a recruiter like Mr Armin does in Bangladesh.

   ____

   ____

   ____

3. Describe what can happen to immigrants who refuse to do as they are told …

   a) in Malaysia.

   ____

   ____

   ____

   b) back at home.

   ____

   ____

   ____

2 Writing an email

Write a short email Jashel could have written to his family about his first impressions when arriving in Kuala Lumpur/Malaysia.

____

____

____

____

____

____

____

____

____

____

____

____

____

____

____

Mediation → SB, p. 64

Your English friend is really frustrated that his family produces so much waste and asked you for advice to convince them of some environmentally-friendly alternatives.
Write an email to him in which you inform him about shopping in zero-waste supermarkets. Use the below information from a website to tell him what zero-waste shops offer, how you shop there and what their advantages are.

Unverpacktläden

Nach einem einstündigen Slalomlauf durch die Regale ist der Einkaufswagen endlich voll. Zu Hause dann auspacken. Wenn alles im Kühlschrank verstaut ist, stehen wir bestimmt mit der gleichen Menge an Verpackungsmaterialien da – viele Einwegverpackungen, Kartons, Plastikbehältnisse.

Ich weiß, eine Möglichkeit ist es, sich dem Konsum total zu verweigern. Eine andere Idee sind die sogenannten Unverpacktläden, die sich dem „Zero Waste“ Prinzip verschreiben. Das Sortiment dieser Läden beschränkt sich bei weitem nicht mehr nur auf Getreideprodukte oder Obst und Gemüse. Es gibt Milchprodukte genauso wie Drogerieartikel, Fertigprodukte und Süßwaren. Oft kommen diese Produkte aus regionalem Anbau, wobei lange Transportwege und Zwischenhändler vermieden werden. Dass du die regionalen Produzenten unterstützt, ist ein weiterer Punkt, in diesen Läden einzukaufen. Regionale Produzenten erhalten eine faire Bezahlung, was nicht heißt, dass ihre Produkte auch teuer sein müssen.

Und es ist doch ganz einfach. Im Laden befinden sich die Waren oft in durchsichtigen Spendern, so dass du genau weißt, was du kaufst. Bring einfach deine eigenen Behälter mit. Damit vermeidest du Einwegverpackungen und schonst die Umwelt. Produkte wie Milcherzeugnisse kaufst du oft in Pfandflaschen und -gläsern.

Sicher dauert es auch etwas länger. Du planst und organisierst deinen Einkauf sorgfältiger und die Waren müssen im Laden einzeln abgewogen werden. Aber auf diese Weise einzukaufen heißt auch entschleunigen. Viele der Unverpacktläden haben nicht nur aus diesem Grund auch ein Café. Frag einfach mal deine Großeltern, wie sie damals im Tante-Emma-Laden eingekauft haben. Sicher ist es für dich eine Umstellung, aber es ist doch gar nicht so schwer.

Global English

A5 **1 Listening: Intercultural communication**

Professional communication faces specific challenges in situations where people from different cultures work together.

a Think of a peach and of a coconut. Describe each in 2–3 sentences.

b Listen to the conversation and choose the sentence that best describes the situation.

- ☐ Michelle and Felix are prejudiced about each other's cultures.
- ☐ The two interns are discussing ways to deal with cultural differences appropriately.
- ☐ Michelle and Felix are very open and do not have a problem with cultural differences.

c How does the coconut and peach metaphor work for Germans and Americans?

Germans – coconut	
Americans – peach	

2 Listen to the conversation again and do the following tasks.

a Write down the 'false friends' mentioned and their correct English translation.

German false friend	correct English translation

b Complete Felix' and Michelle's clichés about and experiences with Americans and Germans.

Felix about Americans	
Michelle about Germans	

c Which examples of differences in business situations does Michelle give?

small talk	
Sie/du	
humour in business situations	

d Explain the "flexible thinking model".

3 Writing a comment → S 6

You have certainly come across people of different cultural and ethnical backgrounds or different countries as well. What cultural differences have you experienced? Did you have any prejudices that turned out to be right or wrong?

1 Word building → SB, p. 68

a Add the appropriate suffix to complete these professions. You may need to change the ending of the word.

-ist | -er | -ian | -or

1. mathematics *mathematician*
2. reception ______
3. science ______
4. dental ______
5. forest ______
6. technology ______
7. bake ______
8. electricity ______
9. direct ______
10. library ______

b Use prefixes to find the opposite to these words.

1. wrap ______
2. agree ______
3. tidy ______
4. engage ______
5. behave ______
6. understand ______
7. spell ______
8. connect ______
9. fold ______
10. polite ______

c Complete the table with the different forms of the words below. Then think of two more (also related to professions).

Noun	Adjective	Adverb	Opposite of the noun (antonym)
strength			
		competently	
			ineffectiveness
	interesting		
		practically	

1 Working with a dictionary → SB, p. 69

Use a dictionary to complete the table about the words from the text.

Why communication skills are essential in the workplace

When it comes to working in a team, it is imperative that each team member communicates his or her ideas clearly. Good communication skills help eliminate misunderstanding and conflict. It is unavoidable that people sometimes contradict each other. In cases when opposing opinions seem to be hard to resolve, it takes particularly effective communication skills to mitigate this conflict.
The danger of miscommunication is particularly high in situations where people from different cultures work together. Intolerance of the norms and habits of another culture – or sometimes merely a lack of sensitivity to cultural differences – can lead to severe misunderstanding and embarrassing blunders. Workers should receive training in intercultural communication to avoid conflict and misunderstanding. To increase effectiveness and productivity, it is essential to implement effective strategies for communication within and across cultures.

	Word class	German translation	Definition in English	English synonym
imperative				
contradict	*verb*			
resolve				
mitigate		*mildern*		
merely				
severe				*extreme*
blunder				

2 Choosing the right word

Some German words have several possible English meanings.
Use a dictionary to help you translate these typical examples into English.

Land	eng
"Luxemburg ist ein sehr kleines Land."	„Nach einem engen Treppenhaus kommt man an eine kleine Tür."
„Nach einer langen Schiffahrt freut man sich, endlich wieder Land zu sehen."	„Der Sänger der Band trug enge Jeans und ein enges T-Shirt."
„Viele Menschen leben lieber in der Stadt als auf dem Land."	„Die beiden Mädchen waren sehr eng befreundet."

A The language of pop music

1 Listening: English as a Lingua Franca → SB, p. 73 → S 2

Listen to the podcast and answer the following questions.

1. Why are linguists around the world gathering words spoken between non-native people? (2 things)

   ____

   ____

   ____

   ____

   ____

2. What are the students from Japan and China drinking in the pub?

   Japan: ____

   China: ____

3. Put in the missing words about Jennifer's experience with discussions in her lessons.

   In my lessons I would give the students something very ______________ to discuss. The students would then ____________ with the subject, using their English. We often had ______________ discussions and the students were ________________ with each other. This way they were ________________________ very well.

4. Where was English used 50 years ago in contrast to today? ____

   ____

5. What language combinations are mentioned in the text? ____

   ____

2 Focus on Grammar: Present Perfect → SB, p. 73 → Talking about the present perfect

Fill in the verb in the present perfect simple or present perfect progressive.

1. I ______________________ (learn) English for 10 years.
2. Many of my classmates ___________ never ___________ (use) English outside the classroom.
3. For centuries the English language ______________________ (change) gradually.
4. How long ________________________ (deal) with this topic?
5. In recent years learning Chinese ________________ (become) more and more important.
6. The rise of English as a lingua franca ________________ (spark) much interest among linguists.
7. The influence of English words on other languages ________________ (grow) over the last decades.
8. Governments and companies __________________ (invest) huge sums of money in English lessons.

B The legacy of colonialism

1 Reading for gist → SB, p. 74–75

a Put the headlines in the order of the text.

The challenge of being critical about colonialism ____

Changed attitude with more knowledge ____

Appeal to talk about the legacy of colonialism ____

People's ignorance about the British Empire ____

Partying colonial style ____

Not focusing on the actual problems ____

Necessity of talking about the British Empire ____

Why railways were built during the British occupation ____

b Note down a list of the problems caused by the British Empire as given in the text.

____

____

____

____

____

2 Words matter → SB, p. 74–75

a Find the odd one out. Cross out the word that doesn't fit in the row.

1.	throw	invite	put on	party	organize
2.	slave	oppression	colonialism	tourism	occupation
3.	unsure	clueless	grateful	ignorant	uneducated
4.	sick	glory	chic	glamourous	luxurious

b Paraphrase the following phrases from the text.

1. the glory days of the early 20th century (l. 7):

____

2. to live side by side (l. 8):

____

3. it breeds a type of contempt (l. 32):

____

4. the chip is on my shoulder (l. 34):

____

5. the necessary national conversation (ll. 39–40):

____

3 Focus on grammar: If-clauses → SB, p.76 → Talking about conditions

Match the sentences with the most suitable ending.

1 You will learn more about the German colonial empire
2 How would we react
3 If India and Pakistan had not been partitioned in 1947,
4 If students talked more about the British Empire,
5 We will see that there is some kind of new colonialism in developing countries
6 If somebody threw a 'colonial chic' party in Germany,
7 The horrible fate of many slaves could have been avoided

A there might not be conflicts between these two countries today.
B they would understand the impact it had on Great Britain itself.
C if slave trade had been abolished earlier.
D if you read the books available in our library.
E if we look carefully at the world today.
F if somebody tried to rule our country?
G people would certainly not know how to react.

4 Focus on grammar: Modal verbs → SB, p.75 → Talking about ability, permission and necessity

Janice's friend has hearing problems, so Janice wants to learn the sign language to communicate better with her friend. Put in *have to*, *be allowed to* and *be able to* in the correct tense.

When I met George for the first time, we ________________ 1 communicate well with each other. I ________ 2 speak slowly to George, facing him directly. In class we ________________ 3 talk to each other but I wanted to help him with some of the tasks. So I came up with the idea to learn the sign language in a course offered by the Open University. Fortunately, you ________________ 4 pay for the courses there.

On the first day of our course the teacher greeted us with sign language but nobody ____________ 5 understand her. She then talked about the importance of sign language and finger spelling.

Do you know that about 150,000 British people ________________ 6 communicate in this way? During our three-month course we ________ 7 do different tasks. In tests we ________________ 8 use gestures and sign language, of course. But I ____________ 9 do many tasks easily as I had often practised with George beforehand. When I walk around town with George now I notice that many people ________________ 10 communicate effectively with deaf people. For example, I think shop assistants should ____________ 11 greet deaf and hard-of-hearing customers . It would make them feel more welcome.

C Teenage problems

1 Word web

Complete the following word web with issues young people might have.

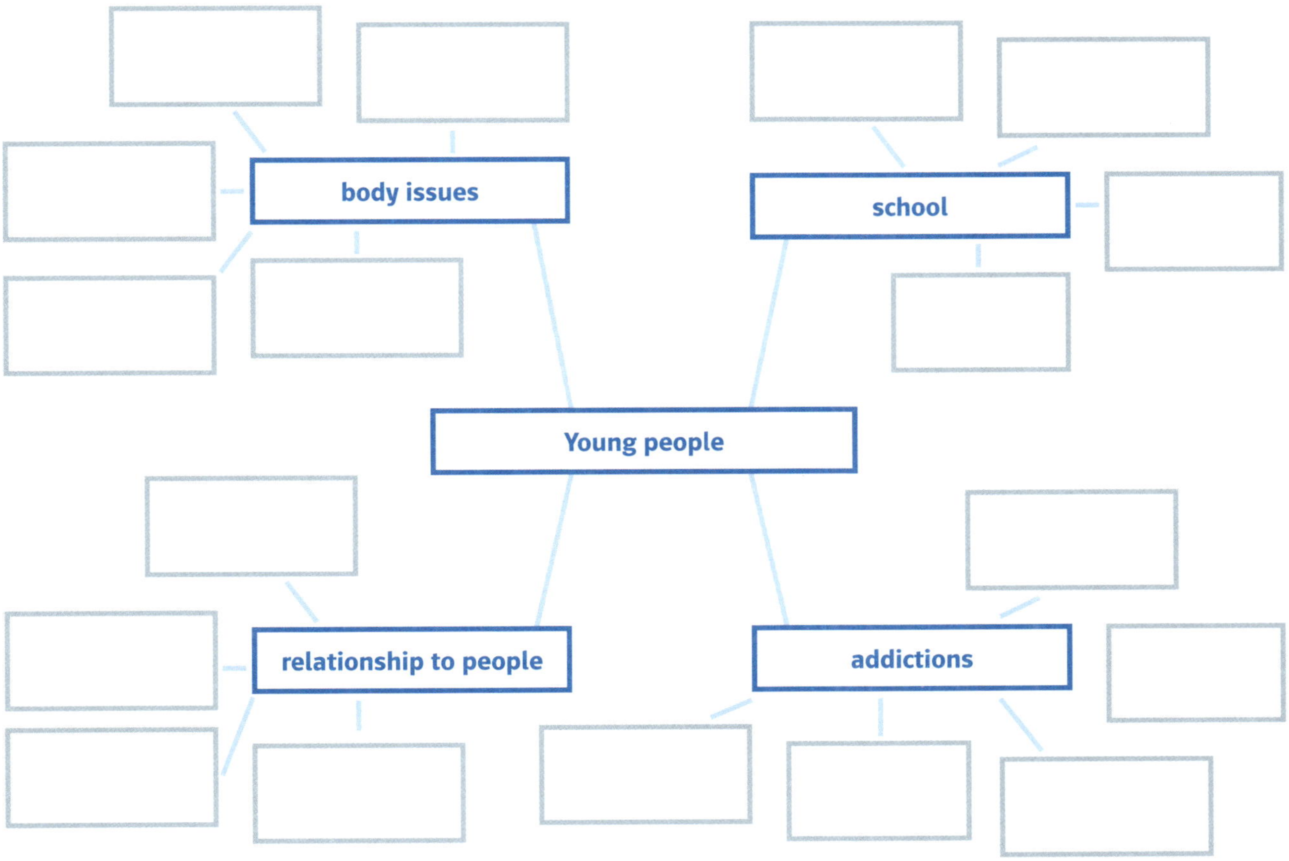

2 Writing a blog entry

A friend of yours has one of the problems mentioned above. You want to help him/her but do not know how. On the internet you found a very useful site where people can ask for advice.
Describe the problem your friend has.

3 Words matter → SB, p.77–78

a Find phrases in the text that are used to describe results of studies.

1. eine Studie/ein Bericht fand heraus, dass	
2. laut der Studie	
3. im Vergleich zu	
4. Forscher führten die Studie von … durch	
5. standen an 5. Stelle	
6. die Abnahme von	
7. höher als der Durchschnitt	

b Use the internet to find a statistic about one of the problems in 1 and describe it with phrases from 3a.

____

____

____

____

____

4 Writing: School problems

Your friend has a problem and you want to help. Complete the chat with possible statements.

I am fed up with school. ☹ Won't go there tomorrow. First this stupid Maths lesson and then PE.

____

That's true, but it was much better last year. We get too much homework now!

____

Would you really help me? How could we organise this?

____

____

☺ I already feel a lot better! But these horrible PE lessons. Why should we do sport anyway?

____

OK. I will come to school tomorrow. What would your parents say if you skipped lessons?

____

D The USA and the world

1 Test your knowledge

a What do you know about the USA? Do the quiz. Then compare your answers with your partner and complete missing words. The first letters, read from top to bottom, give you the solution.

1. adjective to describe Americans who love their country: _ _ _ _ _ _ _ _ _
2. one of the major political parties: _ _ _ _ _ _ _ _ _ _ _
3. the bird that represents the USA: _ _ _ _ _
4. highest court in the USA: _ _ _ _ _ _ _ _   _ _ _ _ _
5. the war Americans fought with the British: _ _ _ _ _ _ _ _ _ _ _ _   _ _ _
6. one of the major political parties: _ _ _ _ _ _ _ _ _
7. take place every four years: _ _ _ _ _ _ _ _ _
8. the people who first lived in America: _ _ _ _ _ _   _ _ _ _ _ _ _ _ _
9. a social media platform represented by a bird: _ _ _ _ _ _ _

b Answer the following questions in key words. Compare with your partner.

1. What countries are the global superpowers of today? ____________________
2. Name areas where the USA plays an important role. ____________________
3. In what jobs do you think people (in the USA) earn most and least?
   most: ____________________
   least: ____________________
4. Can you think of people who went 'from dishwasher to millionaire', living the American Dream?
   ____
5. What goods which are *really* produced in the USA do you know?
   ____

2 Words matter → SB, p. 80 – 81

a There are lots of alternatives to avoid using 'say' and 'ask' all the time. Find words in the text that show how people commented on something.

____

____

b Put in words from a that fit best.

1. The President ______________ the nation how successfully he had managed the disaster.
2. The teacher ______________ how Germany's foreign policy works.
3. Many people ______________ what the postwar order will be like.
4. Please ______________ that you have to check all the information on internet platforms carefully.
5. Economists ______________ that there will be a stagnation in the production of hybrid cars.

Ride, hustle, kill, repeat: The underground cycle gangs of Los Angeles

→ SB, p. 84–85

1 Reading for gist

a Describe the atmosphere in Hope Street before the actual race begins.

b Describe the beginnings of the cycle races.

c Explain what the words "Ride, hustle, kill, repeat" mean, referring to the content of the text.

d Find examples in the text of how the author is trying to make the article interesting and appealing to the reader.

Do you speak internet?

What your online life says about you

→ SB, p. 86 – 87

1 Doing a mediation step by step

a Write an introduction to the text, referring to the addressee and reason for writing this text.

b Scan the text and find key words in the text which are necessary to retell the content.

c Write down one sentence to tell your friend what the text is about.

d Take notes about what you learn about Gretchen McCulloch.

e Summarise the main ideas Gretchen McCulloch is talking about. Write down notes.

f Write one final sentence to conclude your mediation.

The impact of change

1 Trends in the world of work → SB, pp. 88 – 89

a Organise the following words into adjectives, verbs and nouns.

drastic | key | irreversible | progress | deal with | impact | intelligence | trend | advancement | repetitive | tasks | efficiency | downsides | disadvantages | outweigh | convenient | flexibility | adapt | current | decade | artificial | cope with | useful | noticeable | modernise | employees | place of work | important | improve | loss | tedious | computerise | smart | advance | benefit | technological | traditional | reduce | outsource | remote | balance | opportunity

adjectives: ______________________________

____

verbs: ______________________________

____

nouns: ______________________________

____

____

b Use words from the list above to write sentences about each of the pictures.
What is the trend shown? What is your personal opinion about this change?

____

____

____

____

____

____

____

____

____

2 Crossword puzzle → SB, pp. 88 – 89

Across (→)

1. clever
4. the use of machines to do work that was previously done by people
5. chance
7. disadvantage
12. doing the same thing many times, so that it becomes boring
15. distant
16. useful, easy or quick to do
20. a period of ten years
21. no longer having something
22. happening now
23. to arrange for somebody outside a company to do the work
25. to move forward
26. easy to see
27. a person who is paid to work

Down (↓)

2. to change something to make it suitable for a new use
3. powerful effect
6. to make better
7. extreme
8. advancement
9. positive effect
10. to be greater or more important than something
11. a general direction in which a situation is changing
13. cannot be changed back
14. a person or company that pays people to work for them
17. of special meaning
18. taking too long, boring
19. an even distribution
24. work that somebody has to do

1 Describing and analysing diagrams → SB, pp. 90–91 → S 10.4

Complete the sentences to describe and analyse the following diagram.

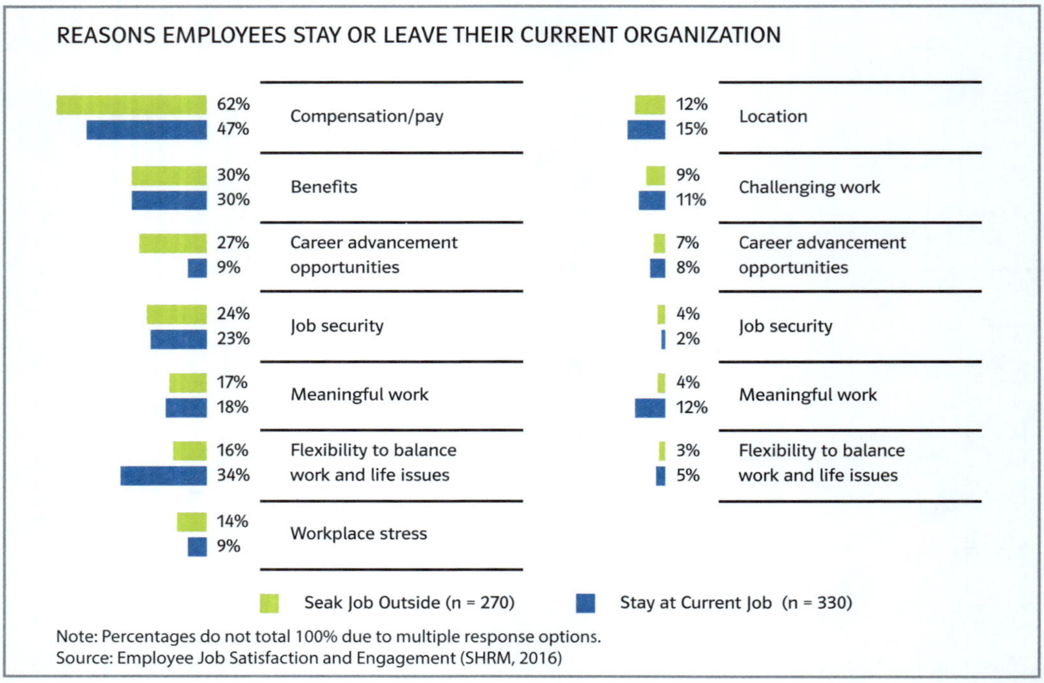

Description

The diagram is about ______________________________ 1.
__________ 2 people from ______________________________ 3 were surveyed.

It is a ______________ 4 consisting of ______________________ 5, each of which has ______________ 6: one for ______________ 7, the other for ______________ 8.

The most ______________ 9 reasons for leaving or staying at an organisation, such as ______________________ 10, are placed towards the top of the diagram, and the ______________________ 11, for example ______________________________ 12, are placed at the end.

Analysis

All in all, we can say that ______________________________ 13. A wide variety of subjective reasons are mentioned and the figures are not conclusive towards any one factor. The diagram should be handled critically because ______________________________ 14.

2 Describing and analysing pictures → SB, p. 92 → S 10.1

Match the following parts of the sentences to describe and analyse the photo.

1 In the foreground there are	A is a production hall.
2 The fact that there are no humans	B windows or doors to be seen.
3 The setting of the photo	C and shiny.
4 No human being can	D clean, cool and artificial.
5 The floor is white	E cold, bright and clear.
6 The impression that is created is	F underlines the impression of a futuristic world.
7 The colours are mainly	G one of a laboratory rather than of a factory hall.
8 The overall atmosphere is	H two production robots, each facing a production line.
9 Some of the robots	I be seen in the photo.
10 There are no	J are working together.

3 Focus on grammar → Talking about describing things in more detail

Combine the following sentence pairs using relative clauses.

1. Many changes contain both advantages and disadvantages.
   These changes are happening today.
   ____
   ____.
2. Changes can be seen in all parts of society. The changes are a result of developments in automisation and demands for more flexibility and comfort.
   ____
   ____.
3. The distribution company has an automated packaging system.
   Its robots were designed and produced in China.
   ____
   ____.
4. My neighbour used to work in a factory. Now he is unemployed.
   ____.
5. The manufacturing contracts are assigned by the CEO. They are outsourced to India.
   ____.

A Digital payment

1 Words matter → SB, pp. 93 – 95

Decide on the word class and find a related word of another word class.

	word class	related word	word class
technologically	*adverb*		
advanced			
cash			
payment			
financial		*finance*	
contactless			
mobile			
bank			
card			
application	*noun*		
secure			

2 Focus on grammar → Talking about the past, Talking about the present, Talking about the future

Fill in the verb in the correct tense.

1. In larger cities in Sweden, Finland and Norway, cash ________ ______________________________ (not use often) anymore.
2. For many decades, these Scandinavian countries __________ __________________ (be) more technologically advanced than the rest of Europe.
3. Since the beginning of the century, smaller purchases ______ _________________ (make) by contactless payment.
4. These days, young people especially ______________ (not carry) cash with them.
5. People from all walks of life now ____________ (pay) using mobile apps.
6. Nowadays, more and more people ____________ (use) prepaid tickets for public transport.
7. Shop owners say that over recent years, the number of criminal offences ____________________________ __________________ (decrease).
8. Compared to before, even the number of bank robberies __________________________ (reduce).
9. According to official plans, Sweden ______________________________ (abolish) cash in the next ten years.

B Way of life

1 Reading comprehension → SB, pp. 96–97 | Tobic 4

Read the text again. Write down what Eleanor says, does or thinks that shows that she experiences the world around her as new or unfamiliar, and briefly explain why her behaviour might seem strange to the outside world.

Passage	What is new or unfamiliar to Eleanor?	Why does this seem strange to the outside world?
l. 5:		
l. 14:		
ll. 23 – 24:		
ll. 38 – 41:		
ll. 45 – 47:		

A6

2 Listening: Multi-family residentials

a Before you listen. What do you know about multi-family residentials?

b Listen to the interview and answer the following questions.

1. Outline the concept of multi-family residentials.

2. Who can live in a multi-family residential? Give examples.

3. What are the benefits?

4. Which characteristics are necessary for living in a multiple dwelling? Which are undesirable?

5. What have been the biggest benefits for Tim?

c What do you think of the idea of multiple dwellings? Would you like to live in one? Say why.

C Internet of Things

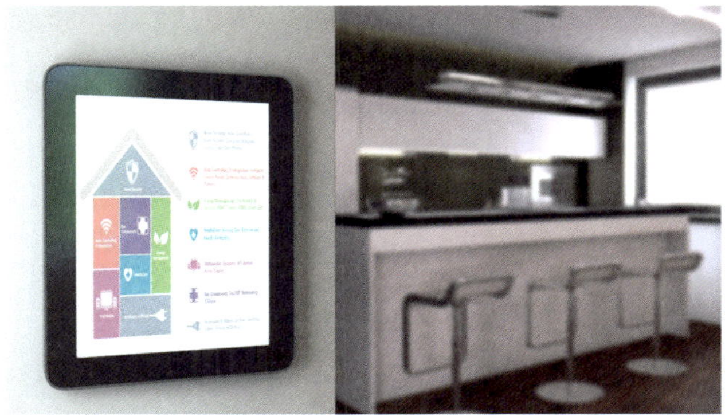

1 Mediation → SB, p.102

Emily, the American exchange student, tells you that there is quite a hype in the US about the Internet of Things. She wants to know if any disadvantages are openly discussed in Germany. You find the following text and summarise it for her in an email.

Die Fallstricke beim Smart Home

Für Hacker und andere Kriminelle bietet das vernetzte Heim, Stichwort Smart Home, neue Möglichkeiten – und Versicherungen ein neues Geschäftsfeld. Über Risiken und Nebenwirkungen der vernetzten Haushaltstechnik. [...]

Versicherer wittern Zusatzgeschäft

Dass Cyber-Security ein zunehmend wichtiges Thema wird, liegt unter anderem am boomenden Internet der Dinge (IoT) und dem Trend zum Smart Home. Rollladen- und Heizungssteuerung per App, Überwachungsvideos auf dem Smartphone, ein Sprachassistent wie Amazons Alexa in der Küche, vernetzte Fernseher und Kühlschränke, die Online Butter nachkaufen: Einer Bitkom-Umfrage zufolge plant jeder Dritte die Anschaffung eines Smart-Home-Gerätes. Besonders gefragt sind etwa ferngesteuerte Heizungsthermostate, smarte Staubsauger-Roboter, Gartengeräte wie Mähroboter oder Sprachassistenten [...]. Gerade Alexa und Co. haben den Trend zum Smart Home kräftig befeuert. Nach Schätzungen des Marktforschers Gartner soll es 2017 bereits 8,4 Milliarden vernetzte Geräte weltweit gegeben haben. Gegenüber dem Vorjahr wäre das ein Zuwachs um fast ein Drittel.

Je mehr Geräte in den Haushalten vernetzt und somit per Smartphone-App oder online aus der Ferne steuerbar sind, umso deutlicher werden auch die Risiken, die sich daraus ergeben. Denn häufig wird bei der schönen neuen Technik das Thema Sicherheit vernachlässigt: Internetverbindungen werden nicht verschlüsselt, Passwörter bleiben auf den Voreinstellungen des Herstellers stehen, Kameras und Mikrophone sind unbemerkt permanent aktiviert. In einem fort übertragen die digitalen Helfer Daten an Geräte, Hersteller und Nutzer.

Für Hacker und Cyber-Kriminelle sind die trendigen Geräte ein willkommenes Einfallstor, das ihnen Macht über das gesamte heimische Netzwerk und alle daran angeschlossenen Smart-Home-Anwendungen verleihen kann. Eine Manipulation der Geräte – vom Auf- oder Abdrehen der Heizung bis hin [zum] Öffnen von Fenstern und Türen – ist dabei ebenso denkbar wie der Diebstahl persönlicher Daten oder Datenmissbrauch bis hin zur Erpressung.

Für Versicherer ist die smarte Technik daher gleich in mehrfacher Hinsicht interessant. Zum einen entstehen durch Smart-Home-Geräte zusätzliche Daten über den Nutzer, die dazu beitragen können, Risiken und Versicherungsbedarf der Kunden genauer zu bestimmen. Eine vernetzte Alarmanlage mit automatischem Polizei-Notruf kann dann zum Beispiel die Hausratversicherung günstiger machen, weil das Diebstahlrisiko sinkt. Zum anderen wittern die Versicherer ein wachstumsstarkes Zusatzgeschäft, weil bestimmte Risiken neu auftreten und bislang nicht versicherbar waren. In gewisser Hinsicht eine schizophrene Situation: Die Technik, die das Zuhause smarter und sicherer machen soll, bewirkt zugleich, dass die Risiken zunehmen und mehr Versicherungsschutz nötig ist.

[...] Das Problem: Die Smart-Home-Geräte müssen einfach in der Bedienung sein. Das schaffen die Hersteller, indem sie auf Nutzerdaten aus dem Netzwerk zugreifen. Wer etwa eine internetfähige, fernsteuerbare Steckdose installiert, muss für die App-Steuerung per Smartphone das WLAN-Passwort eingeben. Das wird dann an das Gerät übertragen und für den Aufbau der Internetverbindung und der Netzwerkverbindung zu anderen Geräten im Heimnetz genutzt und womöglich auf chinesischen Cloud-Servern gespeichert – ohne Kontrolle über Verschlüsselung und Datenschutz am Speicherort. [...]

Aus: WirtschaftsWoche, 2018

a Find the German equivalents of the following terms.

business area ______________________
default setting ______________________
emergency call ______________________
encryption ______________________
gateway ______________________
heating control ______________________
household contents insurance ______________________
insurance companies ______________________
robot vacuum ______________________
robotic lawn mower ______________________
roller shutters ______________________
smart socket ______________________
____
thermostats ______________________
voice service ______________________

b Read the text again and summarise each paragraph.

1. ______________________
2. ______________________
3. ______________________
4. ______________________
5. ______________________
6. ______________________

2 Writing a summary → S 5.5

Use your notes to write Emily an email in which you summarise the most important aspects regarding the dangers of the IoT.

From:	...
To:	emily@america.ex
Subject:	Dangers of the IoT

D Nudge theory

1 Reading for gist → SB, pp. 104–105

Skim the text and write down a subheading for each of the following sections.

ll. 4–13		ll. 55–80	
ll. 14–24		ll. 81–89	
ll. 25–40		ll. 90–100	
ll. 41–54		ll. 101–115	

2 Writing a comment → SB, p. 105 → S 5.1

The introduction should catch the reader's interest and make them want to read on.

a Check which elements should be part of an introduction.

- ☐ An interesting opening (a topical event, relevant statistics, personal experience etc.)
- ☐ A summary of your arguments
- ☐ Your own opinion
- ☐ A definition of the topic
- ☐ A question that you will deal with in your comment, or an outline of what you are going to do
- ☐ A list of counterarguments

b Which of the above can you find in the following introductions?
Underline the positive elements in green and the negative elements in red.

1. In this comment I will be talking about nudge theory. Nudge theory has the goal to make people behave in a way that is good for themselves or others. We need to ask, however, whether it is right to influence people or not. I will deal with this topic in the following essay.

2. When driving into a town a bit too fast, we see a sad face on the side of the road. We immediately slow down to make the face turn happy. This is an example of nudge theory – a theory that has been developed with the goal of influencing people's behaviour, but always leaving them the option of not following the course of action that the nudge suggests. In the end, it is my wish to make the face happy that makes me slow down, and not someone forcing me to do so. The question arises of whether this is appropriate, or if it is a form of manipulation that undermines a person's free decision-making process.

3. Nudge theory tries to influence people to do the right thing – but manipulating someone is never right. In the following comment, I will give the reasons why I think so.

c Which of the above introductions is the best? Say why.

____

____

____

____

How social media is changing language → SB, p.109

1 Words matter

a Match the words from the text with their antonyms.

1 succinct	☐ satisfy
2 evolve	☐ absence
3 malleable	☐ stagnate
4 presence	☐ wordy
5 annoy	☐ fixed

b Read through the text and find synonyms for the following words. The lines in brackets indicate where you can find the word.

influence (ll. 1–16) ______________________

short forms (ll. 21–39) ______________________

normal (ll. 52–69) ______________________

nasty (ll. 52–69) ______________________

informal (ll. 70–84) ______________________

2 Reading for detail

Decide whether the following statements are true or false. For the true statements, indicate the lines. For the false statements, correct them in complete sentences.

Statement	True	False
Because of all these new ways of communication, formal writing is undergoing a change as much as language in general.		
The phrase LOL is just a little bit older than you.		
The hashtag symbol can be found anywhere today.		
The way we communicate on social media is limited to social media itself.		
In social media words can lose their original meaning and are sometimes used in a negative way.		
In the end it is the mass media like TV or the press that make people aware of new word trends.		

Mediation → SB, p.110

1 Summarise the ideas below in English.

1. Das ist nicht der einzige Grund, warum Memes nicht immer nur positiv gesehen werden. Der Betrachter sieht ein lustiges Bild oder einen lustigen Spruch. Doch versteckt sich dahinter oft sogenannte *hate speech* oder eine bestimmte Ideologie.

___

___

___

2. Das Interessante an Memes ist, dass sie sich auf aktuelle Ereignisse oder Personen beziehen, die momentan im Scheinwerferlicht stehen. Diese Komponente ist natürlich auch für Unternehmen und Organisationen von Interesse, u.a. für Marketingkampagnen.

___

___

___

3. Weitere Kritikpunkte werden oft angeführt. So werden Persönlichkeitsrechte verletzt, was zu Cybermobbing führen kann oder Kinder sehen für ihr Alter unangemessene Inhalte.

___

___

___

4. Doch wie entsteht ein Meme? Es kann aus verschiedenen Quellen geschaffen werden, sei es ein Werbeslogan, eine Textzeile eines Liedes, ein Promi- oder Tierfoto etc. Dazu kommt ein lustiger Spruch in einer bestimmten Logik und schnell verbreiten sich die Memes über die sozialen Medien im Internet.

___

___

___

5. Wieder mal über ein lustiges Bild in einer Chatnachricht gelacht? Memes sind heutzutage aus den sozialen Medien nicht mehr wegzudenken. In unserer digitalen Welt sind sie sehr kurzlebig, können aber in sehr kurzer Zeit Menschen auf der ganzen Welt erreichen.

___

___

___

6. Anfangs brauchte man einige Computerkenntnisse, um Memes zu gestalten. Heute gibt es verschiedene Generatoren, die es ermöglichen, noch mehr Memes auf den Markt zu spülen. Leider werden dabei Urheberrrechte in den meisten Fällen nicht eingehalten.

___

___

___

7. Warten wir ab, welche Neuerungen wir bei Memes noch erwarten können und ob die Nutzer lernen, sinnvoll mit diesen Memes umzugehen.

___

___

___

___

2 Put the paragraphs into a logical order.

A diverse society

1 Diversity in society → SB, pp. 112–113

a Define "diverse society" in one sentence.

____

____

b Find words with the letters on the left that describe the issues and challenges of a diverse society.

D ____

I ____

V ____

E ____

R ____

S ____

I ____

T ____

Y ____

A7

2 Listening: Diversity matters

Listen to the radio show and complete the table. Note down what problems these people encountered and how they overcame their problems.

	What made them different?	Problems encountered	How they overcame their problems
Lucy			
John			
Mary			
Luis			

3 Crossword puzzle → SB, p.113

a Complete the crossword with adjectives from page 112.

Across (→)
3. too little space where you can't move
4. sth that can exist for a long time and is good for the environment is …
5. thrilling, fascinating
7. to have lots of work

Down (↓)
1. very beautiful, for example a landscape
2. extremely unattractive or ugly
6. very comfortable, especially in little space

b Find five adjectives for each of the following topics. You can use the adjectives from a, other adjectives from p. 112 and think of more adjectives yourself.

your home: ______________________________

____

your favourite freetime activity: ______________________________

____

your hometown/village: ______________________________

____

4 How green is your house?

Not everybody has the possibility to move into a zero-carbon house. How can you make a house more eco-friendly? Draw lines, write down your ideas and then explain them to your partner.

1 Stating your opinion in writing → SB, p.114

In a blog you have found different opinions on inclusion in schools. Write your opinion on the quotes using the following phrases.

I am strongly convinced | I am (not) entirely sure | I (seriously) doubt | I am (completely) positive | I (truly) believe | Why on earth | To my mind, ... | In my opinion, ... | I agree ...

1. "Inclusive education is a great way for young disabled people to achieve amazing things in their life."
2. "In inclusive education schools can't concentrate on the special needs of those needing them most."
3. "It causes more stress for the teachers and makes the classroom louder."
4. "Inclusive education is just another temporary fashion."

2 Formal and informal texts

What are typical features of formal and informal texts? Put the features in the correct column.

contractions (I'm, they're) | official language | passive voice | writing in third person | simple joining words (also, but) | complex joining words | active voice | abbreviations | personal tone | academic words | signs and emojis | substitutes of modal verbs (have to, be able to) | well-organised texts | slang words | colloquial words | no contractions (I am) | simple modal verbs (must, can)

Informal	Formal

A Migration and work

1 Reading for detail
→ SB, pp. 117 – 118

Complete the word web with facts from the text.

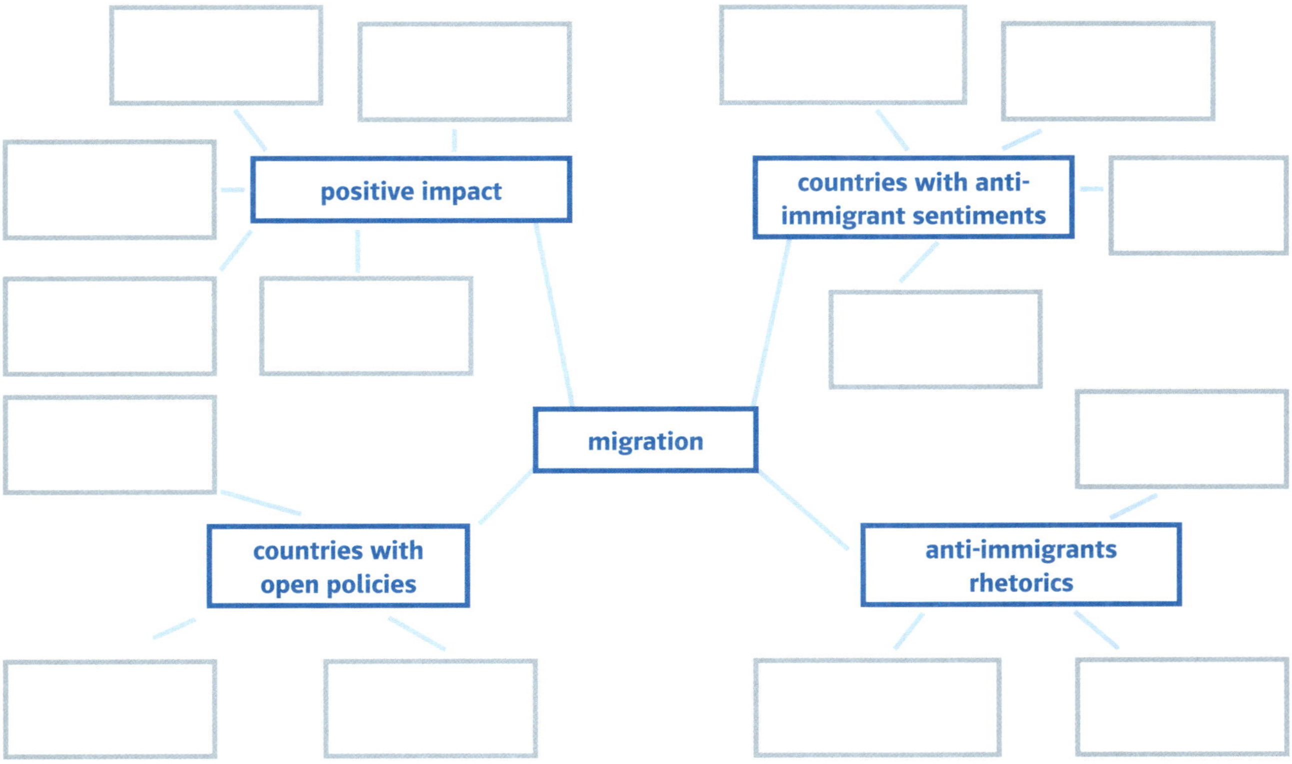

2 Words matter
→ SB, pp. 117 – 118

a Put in one of the following words:

policies | politics | politicians | politically

1. In view of the crisis ______________ of different countries have to discuss measures.
2. The immigration ______________ of EU countries differ widely.
3. Lots of people are not interested in ______________ although it is such an important topic.
4. Many people claim that fairy tales have to be ______________ correct.

b Find the right word for the following definitions from lines 6 to 57 of the text.

1. sending and receiving goods without any restrictions, e.g. taxes ______________
2. the state of not having a job to earn one's living ______________
3. the rate of producing something in comparison to time and money necessary for it ______________
4. the state of having much money ______________
5. the adjective of the study of the population of a country ______________
6. the number how many people are born ______________
7. to make laws less severe ______________
8. protection against dangers like crime ______________

3 Focus on grammar → SB, p.119 → Talking about ability, permission and necessity

a Complete the sentences with *should* or *shouldn't*.

1. Politicians ___________ focus on dividing a country but on uniting it.
2. It ___________ be of utmost priority to the EU to maintain free trade among its member states.
3. Have you heard any news about the new measures? They ___________ be published already.
4. Actually, the government ___________ do something for the prosperity of its population.
5. Our company ___________ have lost so much market share. Could you please check the figures again?

b Look at the sentences in a again and decide if „should/shouldn't" is used to express obligations and recommendations or probability. Complete the table.

obligations and recommendations	probability

4 Listening: Migrant stories

A8

Listen to the reports and answer the following questions.

1. What circumstance helped Amad and his family settle in the UK?

____

2. What does Emine recommend most when migrating to a new country?

____

5 Listen again and complete the table with information from the text.

	Where are they from?	Reasons why they left their home country	Difficulties	Present job
Amad				
Jonathan				
Emine				
Larissa				

B Gender and diversity

1 Words matter → SB, p.120

a Find words from the word field 'equality' in the following categories:

Same word family	
Synonyms	
Antonyms	
Collocations	

b Collect possible reasons why people might be disadvantaged at their workplace.

possible disadvantages at work

ethnicity	

2 Phrasal verbs → SB, p.123

Rephrase the underlined parts of the sentences with one of the following phrasal verbs. Pay attention to the correct grammar. You don't need all the words.

get away with | let down | run out of | look up to | look forward to | get over | put up with

1. Nick is a gambler. No wonder he constantly <u>has no</u> money.

____

2. The teacher did not want to <u>tolerate</u> Julia's behaviour anymore and sent her to the headmaster.

____

3. It took him a long time until he <u>recovered from</u> this unhappy love.

____

4. My mother is my idol. I <u>very much respect</u> her and I am very proud of her.

____

5. Jim, don't <u>disappoint</u> me again. I have relied on your help so much.

____

6. My little brother is so cheeky and <u>is never punished</u> for all the mischief he is doing.

____

3 Focus on grammar → Talking about quantities

Put in *some, any, every, no* and their compounds in the following dialogue.

Teacher: I have ________________ good news for you. ________________ in our class can take part in our trip to London next September.

Sam: Do we have to do ________________, for example book a hotel?

Teacher: No. ________________ will be arranged by an organisation specialising in class trips. We will have to give them ________________ basic information about our wishes, but everything else will be taken care of.

Emma: Will we have to go ________________ together or can we go ________________ we want on our own as well?

Teacher: The idea is that we visit ________________ sights together such as the Tower of London, but you will also have ________________ time to explore London on your own. I haven't decided on ________________ specific sights yet. So you can come to me with ________________ proposals you might have.

Ben: Can't we go ________________ different than London? I have already seen ________________ there.

Teacher: We have already talked about this. ________________ else in this class has been to London before. I am sure there will be ________________ interesting sights for you as well. I have never had a student who was bored in this city. Last but not least, ________________ should inform the absent students about our trip so that ________________ forgets ________________. You can come to me at ________________ time if you have other questions.

4 Working with a video: Horizon, Being Transgender → SB, p.123

V5

Answer the questions about Charlotte. You don't have to write complete sentences.

1. How old was she when she realised there was something different? ________________
2. When did her social transitioning start? ________________
3. What two other things besides wearing female clothes did she do to be perceived as a woman?

____

4. How long will it take to complete her transition? ________________
5. Where is she treated medically? ________________
6. What will she call herself after all the processes? ________________
7. What made the biggest difference to her new life? ________________

C The blue planet

1 Giving opinions → SB, p. 124

You have seen the headlines below in an online newspaper. State your opinions in the comment section using phrases from page 124. If necessary look for information on the internet.

1. Cruise ship polluting air more than all European cars

2. Possible outdoor heaters ban in Paris

3. Injection needles among beach finds

4. Road blocks to prevent pollution from diesel cars

1. ______________________________

____

2. ______________________________

____

3. ______________________________

____

4. ______________________________

____

2 Focus on grammar → SB, p. 127 → Talking about the present

Complete the sentences with the verbs in brackets in the simple present or present progressive.

1. Protesters all over the world ______________ (demonstrate) against climate change today.
2. Many inhabitants of this town ______________ (have) breathing problems. The emissions of the nearby coal-power plant ______________ (get) worse every year.
3. This week we ______________ (organise) a clean-up week. People ______________ (throw away) so much waste that it is high time to do something about it.
4. First thing in the morning, Jack ______________ (go) to the bakery where he ______________ (buy) a coffee-to-go. Why ______________ he ______________ (not take) a reusable cup?
5. Although Phillip constantly ______________ (tell) his parents how important it is to recycle waste, they ______________ (not separate) it.
6. How ______________ companies ______________ (react) to the new law aimed at reducing their carbon dioxide emissions?

D How to live ecologically

1 Healthy eating routines → SB, p.128

a Survey: How often do you do the following? Tick your answer.

	sometimes	often	never
Do you have regular meals?			
Do you normally have vegetables with your meal?			
Do you think about what you eat and assess the possible health risks associated with your food?			
Do you have your meals together with your family?			
Do you drink enough water during the day?			
Do you or another family member cook your own meals?			
Do you avoid sugar, for example in sugary beverages or sweets?			
Do you try to eat less salt, for example in fast food?			
Do you try to limit your meat consumption?			

b Look at your answers. In two or three sentences, write down what conclusion you could draw about your eating habits.

____

____

____

____

____

2 Words matter → SB, p.130

a Write a definition of the following words.

Cosplay: ______________________________

____

webinar: ______________________________

____

Bollywood: ______________________________

____

malware: ______________________________

____

b Think of some other portmanteau words and compare them with your partner's.

____

____

3 A step further → SB, p.130

Complete the text with words from the text (lines 1 to 23) to inform about 'Veganuary'.

Our plant-based ____________ with a record number of 250,000 ____________ this year embraces plant-based diets. Our annual event was ____________ in 2014. Many people also take part without ____________. Our participants take the "Veganuary ____________" and many plan to ____________ vegan. We are also happy to have thirteen new overseas ____________ which have increased our ____________ in the world.

4 Writing about diets

There are different diets people can follow. Find out about the following ones on the internet.
Write a summary of each of them in one or two sentences.

paleo diet: ____

____

freeganism: ____

____

pescetarianism: ____

____

5 Writing a comment → SB, p.130 → S. 5.1

Write a comment on the topic "It's everybody's own decision how he/she wants to eat." Pay attention to the different parts of a comment. Use the following outline to have a structured essay.

Introduction: ____

____

____

Pros: ____

____

____

____

____

____

Cons: ____

____

____

____

____

____

____

Conclusion: ____

____

Swing time → SB, pp. 133–134

1 Put the following events into a chronological order.

- [ ] The mother tells her some people are coming to meet her.
- [ ] Her father tells them to sit down, but only the girl does.
- [ ] The girl looks out of the window and sees the boy outside.
- [ ] The girl goes into the kitchen and sees her mother looking out of the window.
- [ ] The father returns with some tea and says it is a surprise that Emma has turned up.
- [ ] The girl's father tells her that Emma is her sister and leaves the room.
- [ ] When the mother encourages him to sit down again, the boy leaves the flat.
- [ ] The girl sees her father coming towards the house with a boy and a girl.
- [ ] The girl thinks about the things Emma and she have in common and how they are different.
- [ ] The boy and the girl enter the living room.

2 Collect words and phrases from the text which describe the physical appearances of the narrator and her sister, Emma. Then write 2–3 sentences comparing them.

Emma	Narrator

____

____

____

3 To prepare the characterisation of the father, go through the following steps.

a Go through the text and note down the details about how the father behaves.

(ll. 8–9) ____

(l. 20) ____

(ll. 24–25) ____

(l. 30) ____

(ll. 43–46) ____

b Think of words to describe the father's behaviour throughout the scene.

____

Listening: Unusual homes → SB, p.134

1 **Listen to the text again. Fill in the tables with information about Amelia's and Oscar's alternative lives.**

Amelia – canal boat	
location	
size	
time of living there	
reason why living there	
advantages of living there	- -
disadvantages of living there	- -

Oscar – yurt	
location	
origin of 'yurts'	
size	
information about energy and heat supply (name 2)	- -
type of water used	
advantages to normal job (name 2)	- -

2 **There are many different ways to live apart from the traditional flat or house. Choose two of the following concepts and describe what they stand for in about three sentences.**

house swapping | couch-surfing | being a modern nomad | shipping container | tiny house

Trackliste

Topic	Track
1	Track 1: Students' online habits Track 2: The British Accent
2	Track 3: Taking a message Track 4: The gig economy
3	Track 5: Intercultural communication
4	Track 6: Multi-family residentials
5	Track 7: Diversity matters Track 8: Migrant stories

Quellennachweis

Umschlag stock.adobe.com (FS-Stock), Dublin; **4.1** plainpicture GmbH & Co. KG (DEEPOL by plainpicture), Hamburg; **4.2** plainpicture GmbH & Co. KG (DEEPOL / Charles Knox), Hamburg; **4.3** ShutterStock.com RF (Flamingo Images), New York, NY; **4.4** Getty Images Plus (E+ / South_agency), München; **6** www.CartoonStock.com (Jelliffe, Ray), Bath; **7** Getty Images (Getty Images Entertainment / Kirstin Sinclair), München; **8.1** Getty Images Plus/Microstock (iStock / Mekitik_Boy), München; **8.2** Getty Images Plus/Microstock (DigitalVision Vectors / tatarnikova), München; **9.1** Getty Images Plus (EyeEm / Ceres Van Hal), München; **9.2** Getty Images (Westend61), München; **9.3** Getty Images (Moment / Yaorusheng), München; **9.4** Getty Images Plus (Photodisc / Atsushi Yamada), München; **9.5** Getty Images Plus (E+ / jeffbergen), München; **9.6** Getty Images Plus (E+ / alvarez), München; **12** Getty Images Plus (E+ / skynesher), München; **15** www.CartoonStock.com (Carpenter, Dave), Bath; **16.1** ShutterStock.com RF (Gorodenkoff), New York, NY; **16.2** Getty Images Plus (E+ / TommL), München; **16.3** Getty Images Plus (E+ / TommL), München; **16.4** Getty Images Plus (E+ / FatCamera), München; **17.1** Getty Images Plus (E+ / AleksandarNakic), München; **17.2** Getty Images Plus (E+ / PeopleImages), München; **17.3** Getty Images Plus (E+ / FatCamera), München; **19.1** ShutterStock.com RF (SeventyFour), New York, NY; **19.2** Getty Images Plus (E+ / alvarez), München; **20** Getty Images Plus (PeopleImages), München; **23** ShutterStock.com RF (SHUTTER TOP), New York, NY; **24** Alamy Ltd. (rakus), Abingdon, Oxon; **25.1** ShutterStock.com RF (Africa Studio), New York, NY; **25.2** Getty Images Plus (iStock / MachineHeadz), München; **25.3** Getty Images Plus (E+ / SDI Productions), München; **28.1** ShutterStock.com RF (Tim UR), New York, NY; **28.2** ShutterStock.com RF (Maks Narodenko), New York, NY; **29** stock.adobe.com (Daniel Ernst), Dublin; **30.1** Getty Images Plus (E+ / skynesher), München; **30.2** Getty Images (Westend61, Collection: Brand X Pictures), München; **30.3** Getty Images (Tetra images / Noah Clayton), München; **31.1** ShutterStock.com RF (0leJohny), New York, NY; **31.2** ShutterStock.com RF (Warren Field), New York, NY; **32.1** Getty Images Plus (E+ / Pekic), München; **33** Alamy stock photo (Chris Hellier), Abingdon, Oxon; **35.1** Getty Images Plus (E+ / damircudic), München; **40.1** Getty Images (EyeEm / Hieu Nguyen), München; **40.2** Getty Images Plus (iStock / juststock), München; **42** nach: Emplozee Job Satisfaction and Engagement (SHRM, 2016); **43.1** Getty Images Plus (E+ / 3alexd), München; **43.2** Getty Images Plus (E+ / SolStock), München; **44** stock.adobe.com (s4svisuals), Dublin; **45** ShutterStock.com RF (Bodnar Taras), New York, NY; **46** Getty Images Plus (DigitalVision / 10'000 Hours), München; **47.1** Getty Images Plus (iStock / Eoneren), München; **47.2** Andreas Toller, www.wiwo.de; **52.1** stock.adobe.com (Good Studio), Dublin; **53.1** Getty Images Plus/Microstock (iStock / ONYXprj), München; **54.1** ShutterStock.com RF (brandmix), New York, NY; **56.1** ShutterStock.com RF (Monkey Business Images), New York, NY; **56.2** ShutterStock.com RF (Fractal Pictures), New York, NY; **57.1** Alamy stock photo (juan moyano), Abingdon, Oxon; **58.1** Corbis RF (RF / Image Source), Berlin; **59.1** Alamy stock photo (Leon Werdinger), Abingdon, Oxon; **60** Getty Images Plus (E+ / ferrantraite), München;